THURSDAY JANUARY 14 2016

Keith, thanks ⟨ W9-BBZ-210 ing
my poetry book.

Roger C. Morris

CH7

BRAIN WAVES

INTRODUCTION

Welcome to my world. The poems in this book were written over a forty year period from 1975 to 2015. Some of my poems might work better when read aloud, particularly in a *Spoken Word* environment. Others work better when read off the written page, especially if I've presented them in a visual pattern. See what you think. Enjoy.

Roger C. Morris

BRAIN WAVES

ESCAPED POEMS

Roger C. Morris

AMAZON BOOK

2015 Electronic Copyright

All rights reserved, except for review purposes.

ISBN-13: 978-15177952
ISBN-10: 1517796954

ACKNOWLEDGEMENTS:

Many thanks to Mr. Dahl, my high school English teacher, who encouraged me to write, to members of the Minneapolis Writer's Workshop for friendship and listening to my creations. And finally, to Juleen Lund Wangen, my friend and high school classmate who lit a fire under me to get this book ready for publication.

Cover Design and internal sketches: Juleen Lund Wangen

Synthetic poem sketch: Idynne (Kim) MacInnes

Back cover photo: Shawn Morris

Dedicated to my daughter Chelle and son Cory

CONTENTS

CONTENTS

THE VALUE OF POETRY

Art is valuable in any society because it acts like a mirror, allowing people to see themselves and their environment from many different angles. Poetry is a valuable art form because it uses language, the most common form of communication, as its medium.

Prose tends to drain language of its vitality. Words become stale clichés when used the same way over and over. Language is like soil, it must be constantly enriched if it is to produce anything of value.

Poetry reverses that trend. The poet compresses words into meanings and relationships that fertilize the language and produce new mirrors to view ourselves. Take Admiral Richard E. Byrd's story of survival during a deployment to a remote station at the South Pole.

He encounters a loss of electricity and heat when a generator fails. While waiting for rescue from the men at Little America, the base station, Byrd makes a journal entry that contains the following gem:

My thirst was the tallest tree in a forest of pain.

It's a one sentence poem right in the middle of a prose description of a wait for rescue in a life threatening environment. While the prose used to describe the rest of Admiral Byrd's ailments and struggle for survival, fades from my memory, that poetic imagery of the *tallest* tree and *forest of pain* lingers on.

This brief imagery can be very thought provoking. Other poems may humor, antagonize, surprise, enlighten, or have absolutely no affect on a reader.

Whatever the net effect of poetry on readers, it forces them to fill in the missing parts of the response triggered by the images. The *tallest tree* and *forest of plain* in Byrd's story must be constructed in the reader's mind. In art forms such as paintings, sculptures, etc., the parts are already assembled.

The value of poetry then, as opposed to other art forms, is the involvement that it requires of the reader.

Roger C. Morris (February 1975) – Revised March 2015

2

THE CAPTURE OF A POEM

The first step in capturing a poem is to visit a library, a bookstore, or attend a poetry reading. Poetry comes in all shapes and sizes. You might start with contemporary poetry because of the variations in style and subject matter.

A librarian, a bookstore clerk, or a friend may be able to suggest an author to start with, and I will list several of my favorites at the end of this essay. Once you have selected an author, or authors, read through several poems at least one time. If you find any that catch your interest, or trigger an emotional response, read them again, and note which words or phrases you liked. If you draw a blank, don't give up. The problem isn't you.

Go on to a new author, and to save time, try the poems that have interesting titles. If the poems are untitled scan the first few lines for reader hooks. For example, if you found an untitled poem that began with:

Do not pet the feral Cats of Chernobyl!
Might you be curious enough to read further?

Nature endows its creatures with equipment for survival, such as, speed, strength, strategic size, habitat, and camouflage. A poem's equipment for survival, unlike nature's, must make it stand out and be noticed.

In its most basic form, poetry is the use of words and combinations of words to create images or trigger an emotional response, much the same as an artist would use lines, colors, textures, and angles to create a similar response.

When you see or feel this image or emotional response, you have captured a poem. The captured image may or may not be a paragon of clarity. The emotional response might be fear, indignation, confusion, anger, or loathing instead of joy or understanding. In any case the poem has worked. It will survive in your mind for whatever length of time its impact can sustain.

Favorite Poets:
Lawrence Ferlinghetti
(A Coney Island of the Mind)
Sylvia Plath (The Collected Poems)
Langston Hughes (The Panther and the Lash)
And many more than I can list here…

Roger C. Morris (February 1975)
Revised March 2015

SYNTHETIC

I am constructed of all
The latest materials

Guaranteed to withstand
The hardest wear
And still retain
My original shape.

So I find it
Hard to understand why,
When you've washed me,
Worn me,
And hung me up
To drip dry,

You are still
Permanently pressed
Upon my mind...

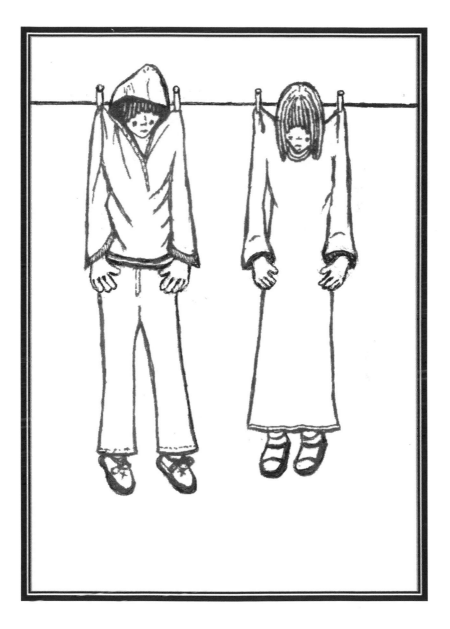

COEXISTENCE

You sit there   on the ceiling

While I hang   from the floor.

Gravity prevents   our collision.

I could crush you,   but spiders I do not fear.

And destruction is not   my mood today

WINGMAN

I lost my wingman
Last night.

We were walking
Down Payne Avenue
When he went into a dive.

Before I could call him back,
There was a MIG
On his tail.
She had no armor,
But was equipped with
Weapons of mass distraction.

They disabled his
Counter-measures,
And he spun out of control.

I knew he was a goner,
So I headed for home.

I'll look for his wreckage
In the morning…

IRON BUTTERFLY

I discovered
A new drink
Last night.
IRON BUTTERFLY!

Now I have an
Urge to pollinate
Just like the
Monarchs in my garden.

As I flit from
Blossom to blossom
The mountains in
Central Mexico
Are calling for me
To migrate.

Bar tender,
One more
Iron Butterfly
Please…

IRENE

With her red hair
And green eyes,
Irene was a
Rita Hayworth
Look alike.

Her impish smile
Masked a sex addict,
Wrapped in a mind
That was deep as a
Sidewalk puddle...

MONDAY NIGHT BLUES

I dig the sound of your sax
Pushing smoke-filled air
Through brass valves, making
Blue notes while I watch couples
Glide around the dance floor.

The women are looking
Better and better as Monday
Night fades into another
Hundred proof Tuesday
Morning…

TOTAL RECALL

Today,
The President
Declared virginity
Retroactive!

Almost as if she thought
Natural resources could be
Reclaimed as easily as
Printing new money.

Tomorrow,
Her declaration continued,
Our minds will be
Recalled.

And
Later, at government
Discretion, strings will be
Attached...

PATIENCE

Patience is a virtue, I'm told.

It worked with the
Compound interest on
My retirement account.
And my lady friend
Enjoys a slow hand.

And best of all, after
Waiting for ten months,
The Check Engine light on the dash
Of my tired old vehicle, finally
Extinguished itself...

GENE POOL

We have contributed
To the Gene Pool,
As our parents
Did before us.

Now, our children
Have added
To the mix.

And I wonder where
The line will end
As we put you
In the ground…

<u>3D</u>

I am equipped
With robotic limbs, and
Brand new organs,
Created with a 3D printer,
Using my own DNA.

And my mind has been
Uploaded to a
Super-Computer
Sitting proudly atop
My robotic torso.

Can functional immortality
Be far behind…

MIRRORS

I collect mirrors. Large ones,

Small ones, wide ones,

Tall ones, any size will do.

My storage space is limited,

So I leave them where I find them.

Except for a miniature that fits right

In my wallet, and follows me everywhere.

My favorite is a two-way mirror in a

Downtown liquor bar. It hangs on a

Men's Room wall above a row of

Urinals opposite the building entry way.

People come and people go,

Oblivious to the grinning inebriate

Standing at a urinal,

Just a sprinkle away...

CHRONOLOGY

My father is old
And drags his shadow
In the dust.

I am an
Aerialist balanced on
Thin threads of reality
That bind my shadow.

But, my son molds
His shadow into mad shapes
That float upon

The slightest breeze…

THE SHORT BUS

I ride the short bus.
Kids laugh at me.

I ride the short bus.
I memorized the value of Pi
To a hundred places
Kids stare at me.

I ride the short bus.
I can play the Minute Waltz
In 45 seconds on my Kazoo.

I ride the short bus.
Now, kids laugh with me…

THE MAN WHO HATES CATS

I know a man who hates cats.

"How can that be?" I asked,
Then listened while he
Explained his feline hate.

"It's in their eyes!
Can't you see the Devil's glare?"

"He's in your mind,
Not the cat's eyes," I replied.

Meeow…

<u>SQUEAL</u>

I run a Factory Farm.
No cause for alarm,
I have no heart.
I was made for the part.

We raise calves for veal.
Can you hear them squeal?
You'd squeal too,
If you lived in their zoo.

Chained in a wooden crate,
Their life's not too great.
But they'll soon have a change of luck,
After a ride in the slaughterhouse truck...

TRANSITION

The soft fire
Of your eyes
Draws me closer
And closer,
Like some creature
In the night.
And your kisses
Are the dawn
That makes me
Eager for the day...

HUNTER

From initial eye contact,
Through smiles
And counter-smiles,
You were my target.

Now at the edge
Of your kisses,
I am drawn taut

Like the string of a bow.
And am at once

The archer and the mark...

MIRAGE

My hot skin,
Stretched erotically,
Has no depth.
Only surface tension,
That mounts until
Your touch releases
A kaleidoscope of
Emotions that stretch
My mind to extend
Your impossible existence…

RITUAL

We light and fuel the fire,
While the ceremony of pounding hearts
Drums blood, lifting us beyond ourselves.

We cling to that naked moment, all too short.
It always ends with us returning
To the flesh embraced below.

We are one, and have become a ritual...

MOTION

I am a traveler, thumbing my way
Down dark roads through bar-rooms,
Bedrooms, head-rooms and far
Corners of my mind, where I
Sit on the web of my memories,
Waiting…

TRAVELOGUE

Dying suffers from a lack of interest,
People do it once and that's it.
What we need are documented
experiences.

Why not take along a tape recorder, or
A sketch pad? When I go I'm
Taking a video camera and
Return postage…

A QUESTION

I heard you telling a friend,
"Love is just
A four letter word!"

I was not asleep on
The sofa as you thought.
Just taking a break from
The all-night party.

Was it wine or weed
Talking, when you uttered
Those toxic words?

I'll find my
Own way home…

CANNIBAL

Like a hungry carnivore
You try to devour me with
Your love while I suffocate
Beneath its weight.

Your relentless teeth sink in,
But draw no blood.
And you shrink back in agony,
Knowing the game is done.

And I retreat in solitude,
With gaping wounds
That none may see...

INSOMNIAC

A moon-mad centaur,
I rush through each night
Faster and faster.

My hoof beats click
Against the dawn
Echoing click clacks
Into infinity.

Finally, I reach out
And clutch night's silent throat
To shake loose the morning sun...

REFLECTION

I saw my reflection
In a store front
Window yesterday.

The tempered glass
Made me look old
In every way.

Until a sniper's bullet
Shattered the window
From two blocks away.

He mistook my reflection
For the man who laid
Him off last Friday…

ASHES

We put Dad down today.
The Vet said it
Was long overdue.

When the organ harvesters
Were finished,
There wasn't much left
For the crematorium.

Now, Dad's ashes rest
In a beautiful ceramic vase,
Perched atop the family piano…

DEATH BED

Your emaciated body weighs less
Than a hundred pounds. A sure
Sign that the Emergency Room
Bed has you in its death grip.

Your eyes are open, but no longer
Shine like they did two weddings
Ago, when we were young.

I'm not a prophet, but know
You'll never leave this hospital.

It's too late for me to say anything,
Except that I'll remember you...

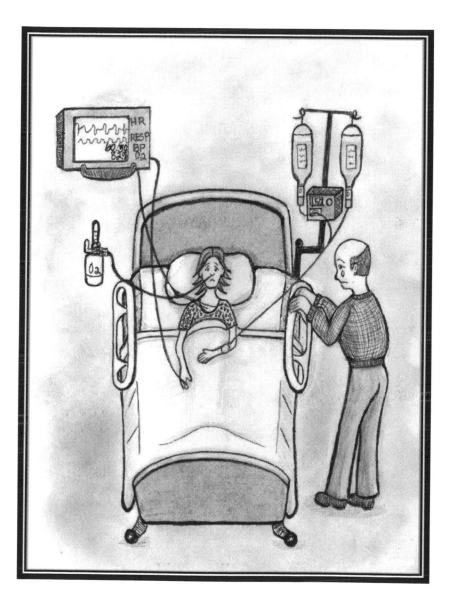

LOST

As a word, Suicide photographs well,
But leaves much unsaid.

Perhaps it's a
Synonym for lost.

John Berryman lost
In mid-flight above
The Mississippi River.

Sylvia Plath
Lost in her oven
At her London flat.

LOST (Cont.)

And now you, lost
At the death end of
A Saturday Night Special.

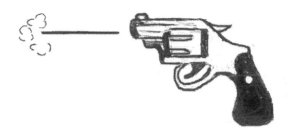

Your casket bound face
Is reassembled
Into a blurred synonym
Of you that my memory
Refuses to recognize...

SUICIDE

I am the savage God.
Come.
Enter my closed circle
And worship me.
Offer me your trinkets.

I collect them all.
Slashed wrists, noosed necks,
Bullets to the brain,
Whatever your gift may be.

And in return,
I am your destiny…

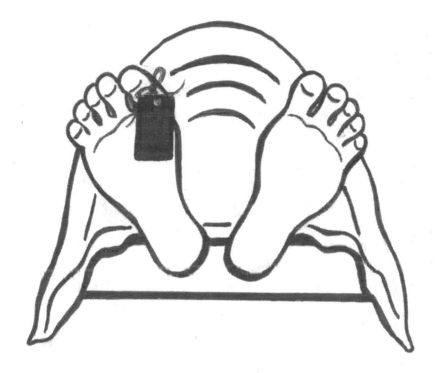

EPITAPH

My brother lies casket bound
Among funeral flowers. A sad
Reminder of twenty-two years.

I look at him and a voice inside
Me says, "He's gone, too soon, too soon."

The words tear at my heart
And tears that others cannot see
Fall in quiet goodbye pools that
Reflect his death while
I am born again,
And again...

END OF THE LINE

I ran out of uncles this morning
When my mother's youngest
Brother passed away.

When I was a boy I saw him eating
Home-cooked Popcorn from a bowl
Of milk and thought he might die from that.

But it was cancer, the doctors said,
That took him down after 76 years…

WRITER'S BLOCK

I am searching for writer's nirvana.
That blissful state where words flow
Faster than I can capture them.

So, I sit at a corner table
In my favorite honky-tonk saloon,
Staring at my laptop screen reflecting
Empty Shiner Bock beer bottles,
As a concerned waitress approaches.

"What's wrong sugar?" she asks,
As I order another Shiner Bock
And try to explain my dilemma.

She smiles knowingly as she leans
Closer and politely offers her condolence
And a healthy dose of cleavage...

ONE NIGHT STAND

I drank you beautiful last night, but this
Morning you came back with a vengeance.

"Breakfast in bed?" you ask.
"I'm not a morning person," I lie.

I spot my clothes on a nearby chair.
And while you go into the bathroom,
I scramble to dress and
Disappear out the door...

BLEEDING LEAVES

Three men hang from bastard trees,
Planted rootless on a hill.

These bleeding leaves
Are not the first to
Hang that high, nor
Will they be the last.

The bearded one,
On the center cross,
Has a message scrawled
Across the bottoms of his feet.

"No deposit! No return!"

It was put there by a clever man
Who crossed those feet
To save a nail...

THE PLASTIC KNIFE

Doctor Manswarm smiles.
His plastic scalpel is poised
Above a struggling patient.

"This won't hurt a bit.
It's just a small lobotomy,
To make you like us," the doctor
Says, as the blade descends,
Singing in its flight,
"Conform! Conform! Conform!"

But the dull blade of society
Strikes only a glancing blow.
"I've failed," the doctor cries.
"The prisoner has escaped.
Come back, I'll try again."

The prisoner looks back through
Many eyes, all sad. "I must go now.
Perhaps the blade was meant for you…"

UPCAST

Livin' high ain't
What it used to be.
Now we do
It artificially.

And my friends all
Tell me I've arrived,
Now that my personality's
Chemically derived.

BLACK

Like the inky sea
That floats the stars,
Black is beautiful.

Like turning leaves of fall that
Burst upon the scene in a sudden
Explosion of color,
Black is here!

MY NEURONS

My neurons were
Firing in the shower
This morning

Before I ran out of ammo, I met
A ventriloquist, a hooker
And a standup comedian

When their neurons were firing
The ventriloquist couldn't keep
His mouth shut while the
Dummy was talking

The hooker couldn't keep her
Mouth shut while her client
Was trying to fantasize

And the standup comedian
Couldn't keep his mouth shut
While drinks were being served

Too bad they didn't
Run out of ammo

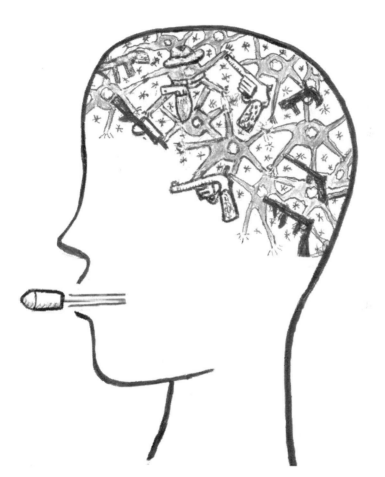

INNOCENCE

There are no lies
In a baby's eyes
There is no guile
In a baby's smile

Where does the innocence go
When a baby starts to grow
Is it lost in a culture
That looms like a vulture?

Greed plays a part
In the ruin of a heart
So capture the child
And remain a bit wild

A child's virtue
Can't hurt you,
But may keep you alive
In your will to survive
In a world gone astray
In a grownup way...

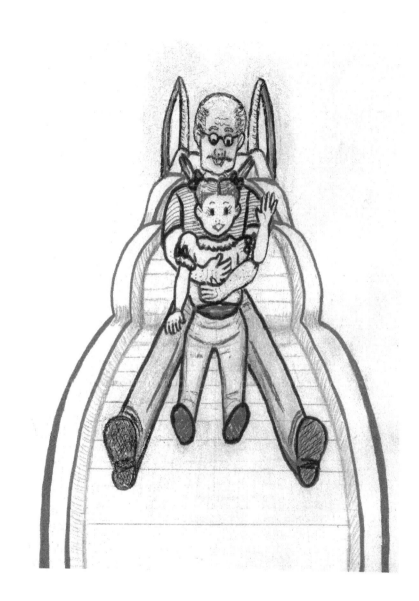

WHAT'S IN A NAME?

My name is Richard Hedd,

With an *H E* double *D D*!

My friends call me Dick, and

Then laugh when I cringe

At the sound of *Dick Hedd*...

Now, when I see my name

In lights, I thank fame for

Making my shame go away...

ALMOST SOBER

We started Friday after work at

CASEY'S on West 7th Street in St Paul.

After a few drinks, loose tongues

Wagged about your old flame,

Now living in Chicago.

You lamented your loss, and the more

We drank the better she sounded.

And the better she sounded, the more we drank.

After closing time, we took a limo to the airport,

And booked a red eye flight to Chicago.

Now, somewhere over Wisconsin at 35,000 feet,

You are maxed out, my Visa card is maxed out,

And I am almost sober. By the way, who

Ordered the airport limo?

CONSCIOUSNESS

According to the latest scientific

Journals, consciousness has been

Simplified into three schools of thought.

The *Neuroreductionists* in their

Traditionalist way, would

Consider me a pack of neurons.

The more popular *Functionalists*

Would compare my consciousness

To a software program.

I prefer a third smaller group, the

Mysterians who are honest, and admit that

The subject of consciousness is beyond

The scope of human intelligence.

Mysterians are often seen wearing

Brightly colored T-shirts that proclaim:

I think, therefore I drink!

WAR OF THE WORDS

Clever marketeers hunch over

Computer Keyboards tapping out

Words of mass distraction.

They create advertisements that urge

Polar families to crave refrigerators, and

And Rubenesque women to yearn

For waif like bodies.

The latest marketing ploy is a word play

Appearing on highway billboard slogans

For jewelry store diamonds:

Sometimes it's okay to

Throw rocks at pretty girls!

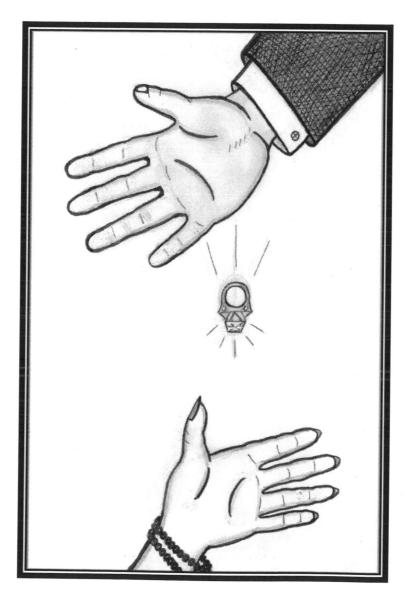

VOCABULARY UPDATE

Dronesplat!

A

Young American GI

Muttered

Under her breath,

As the camera

On her

Surveillance craft

Revealed

Innocent civilian

Body parts

Dripping down

A

Village wall...

SHORT STUFF

***

Where does a mistress go
When her charms lose their glow?
Her lover doesn't care,
He's busy with his kid's new Au Pair...

***

I packed my pipe and took a trip.
The road got rough and I lost my grip.
Tumbling, spinning, terrors unforeseen,
How was I to know my grass was green...

***

My mind is trying to escape
From my body's confining shape.
Maybe someday my body will find
A way to jump outside my mind...

***

One love makes a lover,
Like one drop makes a rainfall...

***

(Tomboy)
Help!
I'm a boy
Trapped in
A girl's body...

CARVE

If you're not falling
You're not learning,
My friend Nikki
Once said to me
As we paused after
An exhilarating ski run

I didn't want to learn
How to fall, so I didn't
Argue the point.

My dialogue is with
The mountain, and how
To let it flow through
Me as I carve my way
Down a ski run...

Nikki doesn't ski anymore,
Since she broke her leg
Attempting to ski down
The Corbet's Couloir,
A famous Jackson Hole
Ski run...

I wonder what she
Learned from
That fall

A MEMORY

I did not sign up

To be your lifeguard.

I was just a concerned father.

I thought alcohol was

Your addiction, but

Then you dragged me

Into a new storm.

You chose a

Needle

And a spoon…

Leaving me with

Just a memory of

Finding you

At half past midnight

Face down on

Your bedroom floor

NOBLE RIDER

The chief lives across a
Busy street from my house.
I see him almost every day.
Bronze face, silver hair
To his shoulders.

Is that his face on the
Buffalo nickels from my childhood?
Or on a giant mountain top
Steed in South Dakota?

Couldn't be!

He's wheelchair bound in my
Northeast Minneapolis neighborhood,
Scooting up and down
The avenue
As the cars whiz by...

THE ADVANTAGE OF BEING A POET

If people argue with me about any

Of my poems, I can always retreat

Behind my trusty shield…

Poetic License!

If my assailant is getting the best of

Me on a poetic issue, I just turn my

Back long enough to draw my shield.

When I rotate back into the discussion,

I'm free to say anything I want, and

If I exceed protocol or good manners,

I just wave my shield with a *Poetic License* smirk.

Then I surprise people by engaging

Them in a normal conversation.

Leaving me with a chuckle,

And them wondering if I'm

Really a poet…

50618199R00064

Made in the USA
Charleston, SC
03 January 2016